PLANETS

by Maria Estes

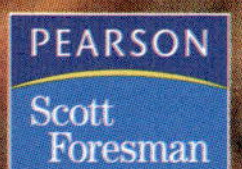

The Universe

The universe is all of space and everything in it. The universe has millions of galaxies. A galaxy is a system of billions of stars, gases, and dust. The galaxy that we live in is called the Milky Way. When you look at the night sky, most of the stars you see are part of the Milky Way. From Earth, it looks like a glowing band of light that stretches across the sky.

If you could look down on the Milky Way, it would look similar to a spinning pinwheel. It is thicker at the center than at the edges.

This is how the Milky Way would look if you could look down on it. Our solar system is just one tiny part of this galaxy.

The study of the Sun, Moon, stars, and other objects in space is called **astronomy.** Early astronomers noticed that most of the lights in the sky remained in the same place. A few of them, however, moved across the sky. We call these moving objects "planets." The word *planet* comes from the Greek word *planetes,* meaning "wanderer."

Other early civilizations also studied the Sun and the stars. Stonehenge is a giant circle of stones in England. Scientists believe that the ancient people who built this had a good understanding of the movements and patterns of the Sun and the stars. Some of the stones point to where the Sun rises and sets on the longest day of the year.

Stonehenge

The Solar System

The **solar system** includes the Sun, the planets and their moons, and other objects. The Sun is in the center of the solar system. All the other objects in the solar system travel around the Sun in a path called an orbit.

A planet is a very large, round object that moves around a star. Earth is a planet that moves around the Sun. The Sun is a star. Planets are cooler than stars. They are also smaller than stars. Planets don't give off their own light, as stars do. They reflect light from the star that they orbit.

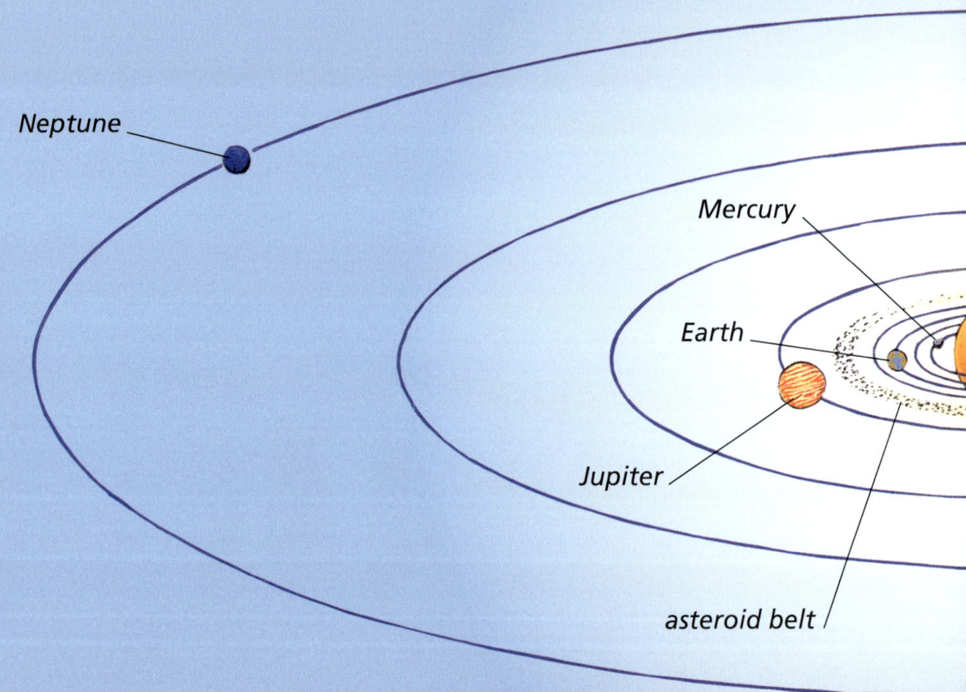

Our solar system has inner and outer planets. Mercury, Venus, Earth, and Mars are the inner planets. They are solid and rocky. Jupiter, Saturn, Uranus, and Neptune are the outer planets. These planets are made mostly of gas or ice.

Asteroids are rocky objects that are too small to be called planets. Asteroids travel around the Sun in a path between Mars and Jupiter. This area is called the asteroid belt.

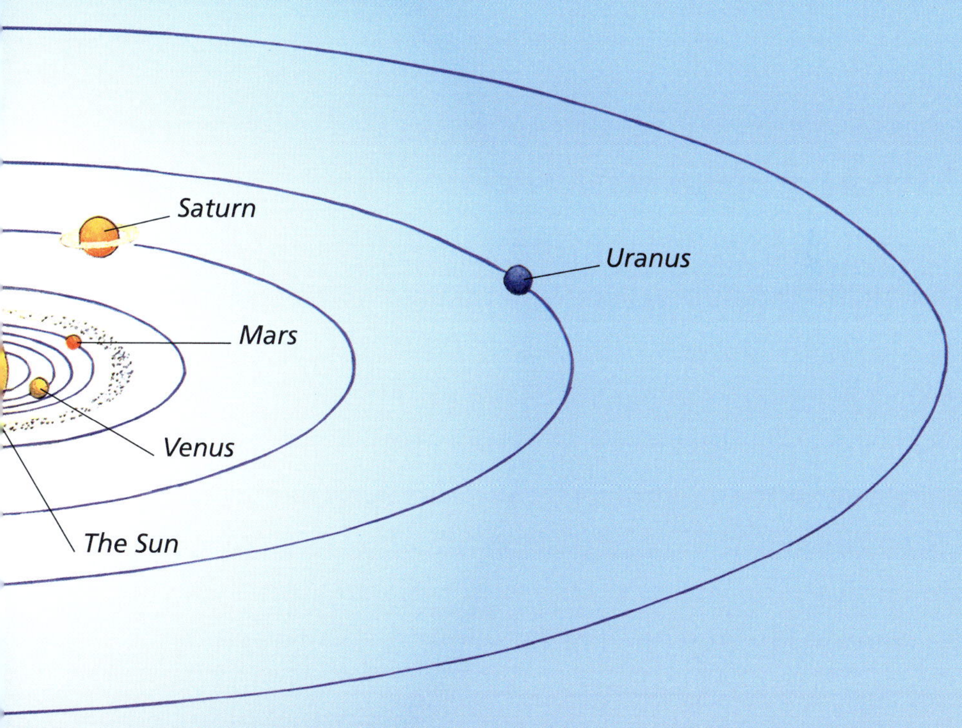

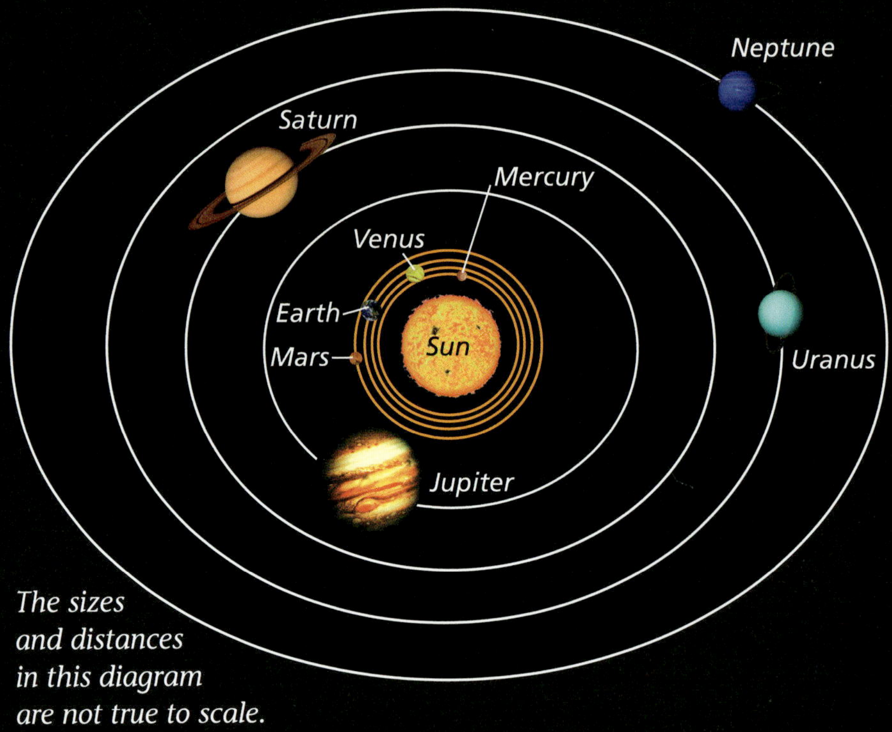

This is our solar system as viewed from above.

What is gravity?

Gravity is the force that holds the solar system together. Without gravity, the planets would move in a straight line off into space. The Sun's gravity pulls the planets toward it. This pull from the Sun makes the planets move in orbits around it.

Look at the diagram of the solar system above. The orbits of the inner planets are almost in the shape of circles. The orbits of the outer planets are not quite as round. Their orbits are longer and narrower than those of the inner planets.

The Sun's gravity holds its gases together in the shape of a ball.

The Sun

Our Sun is an average-sized star. But it is big enough that all the planets and their moons could fit in a small part of it! The Sun, like all other stars, is a huge ball of very hot gases. Energy from the Sun provides light and heat on Earth.

The inner parts of the Sun are much hotter than the outer parts. Scientists have not been able to actually record the temperature of the Sun. However, they believe that the outer part of the Sun is about 5,500°C (10,000°F). The inside of the Sun could be as hot as 15,000,000°C (27,000,000°F).

The Inner Planets

The surface of Mercury has long cracks and ridges.

Mercury

Mercury is the planet closest to the Sun. It's only a little bigger than Earth's moon. The surface of Mercury is covered with huge, bowl-shaped dents called **craters.**

In late 1973, scientists sent the *Mariner 10* space probe to Mercury to gather information. A **space probe** is a vehicle that carries cameras and other tools for studying objects in space.

It is very hot on Mercury during the day. The hottest temperature recorded on Mercury was 467°C (870°F). But it has almost no atmosphere to hold the Sun's heat. This makes the nights very cold. The coldest temperature recorded on Mercury was –183°C (–297°F).

Facts about Mercury

Average distance from the Sun: *57,900,000 km (35,983,000 mi)*
Diameter: *4,879 km (3,032 mi)*
Length of a day as measured in Earth time: *59 days*
Length of a year as measured in Earth time: *88 days*
Average surface temperature: *117°C (243°F)*
Number of moons: *none*
Weight of a child who is 75 lb on Earth: *28.5 lb*

The thick clouds that cover Venus are hot and poisonous.

Venus

Venus is about the same size as Earth. Venus is difficult to study because it is always covered by thick, hot, poisonous clouds. The clouds on Venus reflect the Sun's light. This makes Venus one of the brightest objects in Earth's night sky.

Similar to Mercury, Venus is hot and dry. It also is covered by craters, cracks, and ridges. Venus is the hottest planet in the solar system. Ten Russian space probes have been able to land on the surface of Venus. Several of them sent photographs back to Earth before they were destroyed by the heat.

Facts about Venus

Average distance from the Sun: *108,200,000 km (67,200,000 mi)*
Diameter: *12,104 km (7,521 mi)*
Length of a day as measured in Earth time: *243 days; spins backward*
Length of a year as measured in Earth time: *225 days*
Average surface temperature: *464°C (867°F)*
Number of moons: *none*
Weight of a child who is 75 lb on Earth: *68.25 lb*

Earth rotates around its axis every twenty-four hours. Half of Earth is always in darkness.

Earth

Earth is the largest rocky planet in our solar system. It is colder at night and warmer during the day. No other planet in the solar system has any liquid water on its surface. Much of Earth's surface is covered with water.

The atmosphere is a layer of gas. Earth has a different atmosphere than other planets have. The atmosphere is about 150 kilometers (93 miles) thick. The gases in the atmosphere block some of the Sun's harmful rays. Some of these gases are nitrogen, oxygen, and carbon dioxide. Plants and animals need water and these gases to live. Earth is the only planet in the solar system that is known to support life.

Facts about Earth

Average distance from the Sun: *149,600,000 km (93,000,000 mi)*
Diameter: *12,756 km (7,926 mi)*
Length of a day as measured in Earth time: *24 hours*
Length of a year as measured in Earth time: *365 days*
Average surface temperature: *15°C (59°F)*
Number of moons: *1*
Weight of a child who is 75 lb on Earth: *75 lb*

The Moon

An astronaut walks on the Moon.

A moon is a natural satellite of a planet. A **satellite** is an object that travels around another object in space. Moons orbit planets, just as planets orbit the Sun. Gravity keeps moons traveling in orbits around planets.

Earth's moon is about one-fourth the size of Earth. The Moon has no air, water, or atmosphere.

The country that was known as the Soviet Union sent the first man-made satellite, called *Sputnik 1*, into space in 1957. In 1961, a Soviet cosmonaut named Yuri Gagarin became the first person in space. In 1969, Americans Neil Armstrong and Buzz Aldrin were the first people to walk on the Moon.

Facts about Earth's Moon

Average distance from Earth: *385,000 km (239,000 mi)*
Diameter: *3,475 km (2,159 mi)*
Time it takes to travel around Earth: *27.3 days*
Range of temperatures: *–233°C to 123°C (–387°F to 253°F)*
Weight of a child who is 75 lb on Earth: *12 lb*

Mars

Astronomers have nicknamed Mars the "Red Planet." The rocks and dirt that cover the surface of Mars contain a mineral called iron oxide. Iron oxide is rust. Mars and the dust that swirls around it are a rusty, red color.

Mars has two moons called Phobos and Deimos. Phobos is very close to Mars. It is only about 6,000 km (3,700 mi) away from Mars. That is much closer than the Moon is to Earth. Earth's moon is 385,000 km (239,000 mi) from Earth.

The atmosphere on Mars has very little oxygen. No plants or animals that need oxygen to live could survive on Mars. Strong winds can cause huge dust storms. The red dust that covers the planet is blown around. Reddish-pink clouds often surround the entire planet.

Facts about Mars

Average distance from the Sun: *227,900,000 km (141,600,000 mi)*
Diameter: *6,794 km (4,222 mi)*
Length of a day as measured in Earth time: *25 hours*
Length of a year as measured in Earth time: *687 days*
Average surface temperature: *–63°C (–81°F)*
Number of moons: *2*
Weight of a child who is 75 lb on Earth: *28.5 lb*

Ice caps cover small areas on Mars. There are also many volcanoes and canyons on Mars. The Valles Marineris canyon is more than 4,000 km (1,864 mi) long. That's about the same as the distance from New York City to Los Angeles.

The first space probe to land on Mars was called *Viking I*. In 2004, two vehicles called *Spirit* and *Opportunity* landed on Mars. These robotlike machines gathered samples, such as dirt and rocks, and sent information about them back to Earth.

Opportunity

Jupiter, Saturn, And Uranus

Great Red Spot

Jupiter

Jupiter is the largest planet in the solar system. It is a gas giant. This means that it is made mostly of gas, not rock. Space probes have flown by Jupiter to get information. However, they are not able to land on Jupiter. It does not have any solid surface.

The gases in Jupiter's atmosphere are mostly hydrogen and helium. Jupiter's atmosphere has a weather system called the Great Red Spot. This huge storm has been going on for more than three hundred years! Jupiter has rings around it, but they are too thin and dark to be seen from Earth.

Facts about Jupiter

Average distance from the Sun: *778,400,000 km (484,000,000 mi)*
Diameter: *142,984 km (88,846 mi)*
Length of a day as measured in Earth time: *10 hours*
Length of a year as measured in Earth time: *12 years*
Average surface temperature: *–148°C (–234°F)*
Number of moons: *at least 63*
Rings: *yes*
Weight of a child who is 75 lb on Earth: *160.5 lb*

Colorful yellow, orange, red, and white clouds swirl around Jupiter.

Io

Jupiter's largest moons are Io, Europa, Ganymede, and Callisto. They are about the same size as Earth's moon.

Io has many active volcanoes. They give off a gas that appears as different shades of yellow, orange, and green.

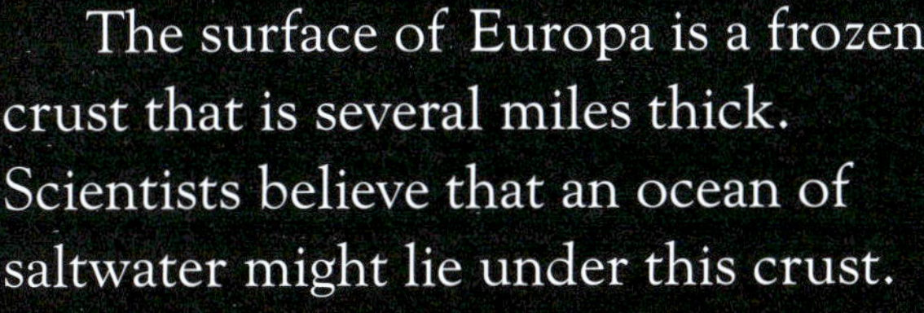

The surface of Europa is a frozen crust that is several miles thick. Scientists believe that an ocean of saltwater might lie under this crust.

Ganymede is the largest moon in the solar system. It is even bigger than Mercury and Pluto.

Callisto is covered with craters. Scientists think that there might be a frozen ocean far below its rocky crust.

Europa

Ganymede

Callisto

Saturn

Saturn is a gas giant made of mostly hydrogen and helium. Saturn is a very large planet—only Jupiter is larger. It is a gigantic ball of gases that contains very little solid matter.

Saturn is surrounded by rings. In 1981, the *Voyager* space probe collected information about the particles that make up the rings. These particles can be as small as grains of sand or as large as boulders. They are probably made of ice, dust, and chunks of rock.

Galileo's Handles

Galileo thought Saturn had handles when he first saw it through his telescope. The handles were the colorful rings that surround Saturn.

Facts about Saturn

Average distance from the Sun: *1,426,700,000 km (885,900,000 mi)*
Diameter: *120,536 km (74,897 mi)*
Length of a day as measured in Earth time: *11 hours*
Length of a year as measured in Earth time: *29 years*
Average surface temperature: *–178°C (–288°F)*
Number of moons: *at least 34*
Rings: *yes*
Weight of a child who is 75 lb on Earth: *55.5 lb*

Moons of Saturn

Astronomers have discovered that Saturn has at least thirty-three moons. Some are small chunks of ice with odd shapes, such as Pan and Atlas. Others are medium-sized round balls, such as Dione and Rhea. Titan, Saturn's largest moon, is even larger than Mercury and Pluto. Titan is the only moon in the solar system that has an atmosphere.

Uranus

Uranus was the first planet discovered using a telescope. This planet is a gas giant. Its atmosphere is made of mostly hydrogen, helium, and methane. Uranus is so cold that the methane in the atmosphere is a liquid. Tiny drops of methane form clouds that surround the planet. These clouds make Uranus a fuzzy blue-green color.

The rings of Uranus are dark and difficult to see from Earth even with powerful telescopes. In fact, astronomers didn't know that Uranus had rings until they were discovered by a space probe in 1977.

Uranus travels around the Sun on its side. Scientists think that an object as large as Earth might have crashed into the planet when the solar system was still forming. This might have knocked Uranus onto its side.

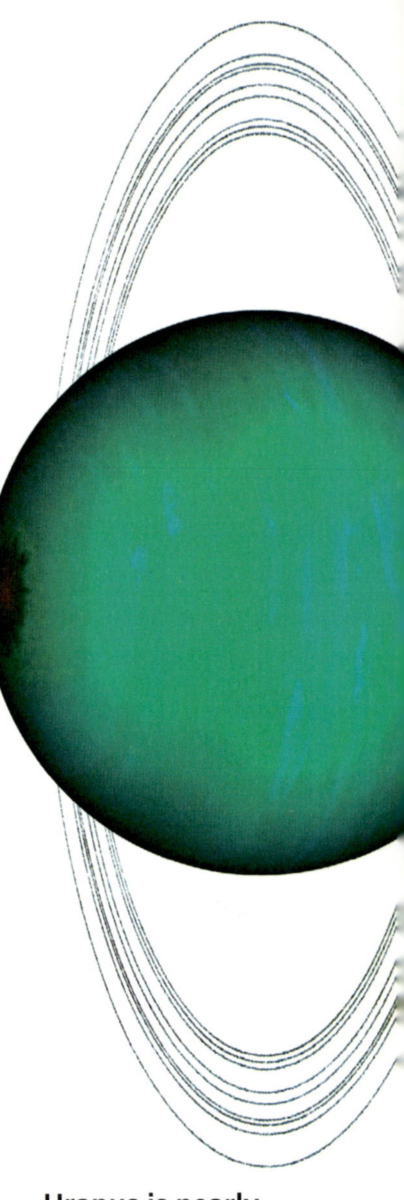

Uranus is nearly 2 billion miles away from the Sun. The cameras on *Voyager 2* had to be adjusted to take photographs in such dim light.

The Moons of Uranus

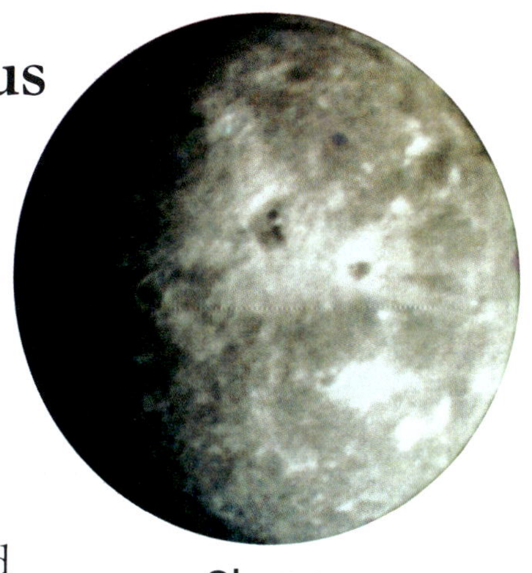

Oberon

Scientists know that Uranus has at least twenty-seven moons. More may be discovered in the future. *Voyager 2* is the only space probe to fly near Uranus. When it flew past the planet in 1986, it discovered ten small moons that astronomers had not known about. The moons are all small to medium-sized. The larger moons have deep valleys and craters.

Arial

Miranda

Facts about Uranus

Average distance from the Sun: *2,871,000,000 km (1,784,000,000 mi)*
Diameter: *51,118 km (31,763 mi)*
Length of a day as measured in Earth time: *17 hours; spins backward*
Length of a year as measured in Earth time: *84 years*
Average surface temperature: *–216°C (–357°F)*
Number of moons: *at least 27*
Rings: *yes*
Weight of a child who is 75 lb on Earth: *64.5 lb*

Neptune And Beyond

Neptune

Neptune is the smallest of the gas giants, but it's still enormous. If it were hollow, sixty objects the size of Earth could fit inside! Neptune can't be seen without a telescope.

The force of gravity between the Sun and the outer planets is weaker than the force of gravity among the Sun and the inner planets. Since Neptune is so far away from the Sun, its orbit is very long. It takes more than one hundred Earth years for Neptune to circle the Sun one time.

Neptune is very windy. Neptune's winds blew a huge storm called the Great Dark Spot across the planet.

Facts about Neptune

Average distance from the Sun: *4,498,300,000 km (2,795,000,000 mi)*
Diameter: *49,528 km (30,775 mi)*
Length of a day as measured in Earth time: *16 hours*
Length of a year as measured in Earth time: *165 years*
Average surface temperature: *–214°C (–353°F)*
Number of moons: *at least 13*
Rings: *yes*
Weight of a child who is 75 lb on Earth: *82.5 lb*

On Neptune, the methane gas in the atmosphere makes the planet look very blue.

In the 1800s, British astronomer John Couch Adams noticed that Uranus's orbit was not following the path he thought it should. He thought that the force of gravity between Uranus and another, undiscovered planet might be the cause.

At the same time, a man named Urbain Leverrier calculated the location and size of the other planet. In 1846, an astronomer named Johann Galle pointed his telescope where Leverrier predicted the planet would be. There was Neptune!

The Moons of Neptune

Triton

Neptune has at least thirteen moons. The largest is called Triton. Astronomers think that Triton may have formed farther away from the Sun and was grabbed by Neptune's gravity.

Pluto, A Dwarf Planet

In 1930, Clyde Tombaugh discovered a small, rocky object whose orbit is sometimes beyond that of Neptune. This object is called Pluto. Until 2006, Pluto was considered the ninth planet. But Pluto is different from the eight planets in several ways. Now scientists refer to Pluto as a dwarf planet. A dwarf planet is a small, ball–shaped object that revolves around the Sun.

Pluto has one moon. It is called Charon. Charon is very close to Pluto and is only slightly smaller. This makes many astronomers think of them as a double planet system. Astronomers also believe that Pluto and Charon may share the same atmosphere when their orbits bring them closest to the Sun.

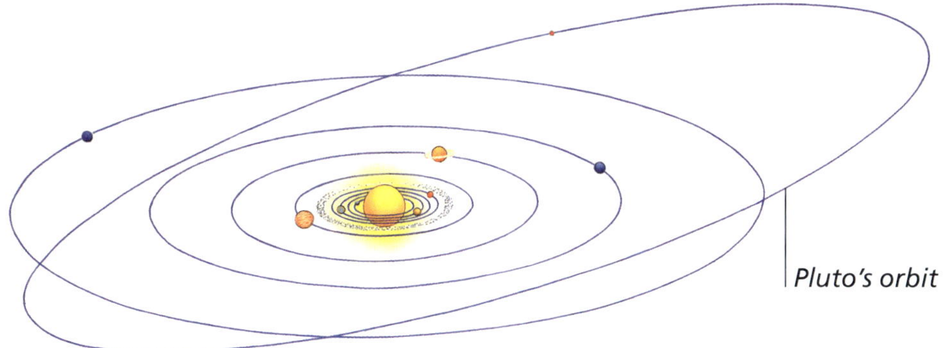

Look at the diagram above. The other planets all travel around the Sun at the same angle. Pluto's orbit is tilted. It takes 248 years for Pluto to travel around the Sun. For twenty of those years, Pluto is closer to the Sun than Neptune. This won't happen again until the year 2237.

Sedna

Sedna

Is Sedna a dwarf planet? Sedna was first seen in 2003. It is the largest object discovered in the solar system since Pluto was spotted in 1930. Sedna is about 84 billion miles away from the Sun. Because of that great distance, it has a temperature of –240°C. Sedna is red, just as Mars is. Sedna is not the only object that astronomers have seen beyond Pluto. However, all the others seem to be too small to be planets.

Spacecraft have landed on or passed by every planet. Space probes might land on Pluto one day. Will that be the end of our exploration? Probably not. With perhaps 50 billion solar systems in the Milky Way alone, it seems that space exploration has only just begun!

Glossary

astronomy	the study of the Sun, Moon, stars, and other objects in space
craters	bowl-shaped dents on the surface of planets and their moons
galaxy	a system of billions of stars, gases, and dust
satellite	an object that travels around another object in space
solar system	a system that includes the Sun, the planets, their moons, and other objects
space probe	a vehicle that carries cameras and other tools for studying objects in space
universe	all of space and everything in it